BABY & Me™
By Marimo Ragawa
Only $8.99
Shojo Beat Manga
BABY & Me
Baby & Me 1
Story & Art by
Marimo Ragawa
1
Young Takuya has it tough. After his mother passed away it has been his job to take care of his baby brother Minoru while their father, Harumi, works long hours. "All work and no play" has Takuya incredibly frustrated and resentful of his little brother. Will Takuya find it in his heart to love the brother who is causing him so much grief?!
Shojo Beat
MANGA from the HEART
On sale at:
www.shojobeat.com
Also available at your local bookstore and comic store.
Akachan to Boku © Marimo Ragawa 1991/HAKUSENSHA, Inc.
RATED T FOR TEEN
VIZ media
www.viz.com

Skip·Beat!™
By Yoshiki Nakamura
Kyoko Mogami followed her true love Sho to Tokyo to support him while he made it big as an idol. But he's casting her out now that he's famous! Kyoko won't suffer in silence— she's going to get her sweet revenge by beating Sho in show biz!
Shojo Beat Manga
Skip·Beat!
Yoshiki Nakamura
1
Shojo Beat™
MANGA from the HEART
Only $8.99
On sale at:
www.shojobeat.com
Also available at your local bookstore and comic store.
Skip·Beat! © Yoshiki Nakamura 2002/HAKUSENSHA, Inc.
Covers subject to change.
RATED T TEEN
VIZ media
www.viz.com

Kaze Hikaru™
By Taeko Watanabe
In 1863, samurai of all walks of life flock to Kyoto in the hope of joining the Mibu-Roshi–a band of warriors united around their undying loyalty to the Shogunate system. In time, this group would become one of the greatest movements in Japanese history…the Shinsengumi!
Into this fierce milieu steps Kamiya Seizaburo, a young warrior. But what no one suspects is that Seizaburo is actually a girl in disguise.
Shojo Beat Manga
Kaze Hikaru
1
Story & Art by
Taeko Watanabe
Only $8.99
Shojo Beat™
MANGA from the HEART
On sale at:
www.shojobeat.com
Also available at your local bookstore and comic store.
Kaze Hikaru © 1997 Taeko WATANABE/Shogakukan Inc.
RATED T+ FOR OLDER TEEN
viz media
www.viz.com

Godchild™
By Kaori Yuki
Deep in the heart of 19th Century London, a young nobleman named Cain walks the shadowy cobblestone streets of the aristocratic society into which he was born. With Riff, his faithful manservant, Cain investigates his father's alleged involvement with a secret organization known as Delilah.
Shojo Beat Manga
Godchild
Kaori Yuki
Only $8.99
Shojo Beat
MANGA from the HEART
On sale at:
www.shojobeat.com
Also available at your local bookstore and comic store.
God Child © Kaori Yuki 2001/HAKUSENSHA, Inc.
RATED T+ FOR OLDER TEEN
viz media
www.viz.com

D+T $5.65 6/07

VAMPIRE KNIGHT
Vol. 2
The Shojo Beat Manga Edition

This manga contains material that was originally published in English in *Shojo Beat* magazine, December 2006–February 2007 issues.

STORY AND ART BY
MATSURI HINO

Translation & English Adaptation/Tomo Kimura
Touch-up Art & Lettering/Mark McMurray & George Caltsoudas
Graphic Design/Amy Martin
Editor/Nancy Thistlethwaite

Managing Editor/Megan Bates
Editorial Director/Elizabeth Kawasaki
Editor in Chief, Books/Alvin Lu
Editor in Chief, Magazines/Marc Weidenbaum
Sr. Director of Acquisitions/Rika Inouye
Sr. VP of Marketing/Liza Coppola
Exec. VP of Sales & Marketing/John Easum
Publisher/Hyoe Narita

Printed in Canada

Published by VIZ Media, LLC
P.O. Box 77010
San Francisco, CA 94107

Shojo Beat Manga Edition
10 9 8 7 6 5 4 3 2 1
First printing, May 2007

RATED T+ FOR OLDER TEEN

PARENTAL ADVISORY
VAMPIRE KNIGHT is rated T+ for Older Teen and is recommended for ages 16 and up. This volume contains sexual themes and violence.

store.viz.com

Matsuri Hino burst onto the manga scene with her series *Kono Yume ga Sametara* (When This Dream Is Over), which was published in *LaLa DX* magazine. Hino was a manga artist a mere nine months after she decided to become one.

With the success of her popular series *Toraware no Minoue* (Captive Circumstance), and *MeruPuri*, Hino has established herself as a major player in the world of shojo manga. *Vampire Knight* is currently serialized in *LaLa* and *Shojo Beat* magazines.

Hino enjoys creative activities and has commented that she would have been either an architect or an apprentice to traditional Japanese craft masters if she had not become a manga artist.

夜刈十牙

Yagari Toga

Yagari is a combination of *ya*, meaning "night," and *gari*, meaning "to harvest." *Toga* means "ten fangs."

Terms

Night Class/Kettle Club: This is a pun. When written differently in Japanese, "Night Class" can also mean "Kettle Club."

-sama: The suffix *sama* is used in formal address for someone who ranks higher in the social hierarchy. The vampires call their leader "Kaname-sama" only when they are among their own kind.

-sensei: This suffix is used for respected professionals, such as teachers, doctors, and mangaka.

yanki: A *yanki* is a juvenile delinquent or young gangster.

早園瑠佳

Souen Ruka

In *Ruka*, the *ru* means "lapis lazuli" while the *ka* means "good-looking," or "beautiful." The *sou* in Ruka's surname, *Souen*, means "early," but this kanji also has an obscure meaning of "strong fragrance." The *en* means "garden."

一条 拓麻

Ichijo Takuma

Ichijo can mean a "ray" or "streak." The kanji for *Takuma* is a combination of *taku*, meaning "to cultivate" and *ma*, which is the kanji for *asa*, meaning "hemp" or "flax," a plant with blue flowers.

支葵千里

Shiki Senri

Shiki's last name is a combination of *shi*, meaning "to support" and *ki*, meaning "mallow"—a flowering plant with pink or white blossoms. The *ri* in *Senri* is a traditional Japanese unit of measure for distance, and one *ri* is about 2.44 miles. Senri means "1,000 *ri*."

玖蘭枢

Kuran Kaname

Kaname means "hinge" or "door." The kanji for his last name is a combination of the old-fashioned way of writing *ku*, meaning "nine," and *ran*, meaning "orchid": "nine orchids."

藍堂英

Aido Hanabusa

Hanabusa means "petals of a flower." *Aido* means "indigo temple." In Japanese, the pronunciation of *Aido* is very close to the pronunciation of the English word *idol*.

架院暁

Kain Akatsuki

Akatsuki means "dawn," or "day-break." In *Kain, ka* is a base or support, while *in* denotes a building that has high fences around it, such as a temple or school.

EDITOR'S NOTES

Characters

Matsuri Hino puts careful thought into the names of her characters in *Vampire Knight*, so in each chapter of *Shojo Beat* magazine you'll find an explanation of the kanji for one character's name. Below is the collection of names that have run in *Shojo Beat* through volume 2. Each character's name is presented family name first, per the kanji reading.

黒主優姫

Cross Yuki

Yuki's last name, *Kurosu*, is the Japanese pronunciation of the English word "cross." However, the kanji has a different meaning—*kuro* means "black" and *su* means "master." Her first name is a combination of *yuu*, meaning "tender" or "kind," and *ki*, meaning "princess."

錐生零

Kiryu Zero

Zero's first name is the kanji for *rei*, meaning "zero." In his last name, *Kiryu*, the *ki* means "auger" or "drill," and the *ryu* means "life."

To those who give me the power to draw my manga, my readers.
To my editor in faraway Tokyo, who always supports me when I get tediously stubborn and retrospective.
To O. Mio-sama, K. Midori-sama, and M. Kaoru-sama, who help me with my manuscripts.
To my childhood friend F. Natsuki-sama, who gracefully lets me use Ichijo-senpai's name.
And to my mother and my dear friends who always help me at various times.

I thank you all from the bottom of my heart! I've got to do better!! Yeah.

樋野まつり
Matsuri Hino

ANOTHER CHOICE (EIGHTH NIGHT)

VAMPIRES COVERED IN BLOOD ARE PROHIBITED FROM ENTERING THIS PAGE/END

KANAME... (NINTH NIGHT)

LISTEN!
THE VAMPIRE KIDS WHO ARE IN THE NIGHT CLASS HAVE A LOT OF PRIDE! THEY'RE FRESH AND ARROGANT!
EEK!
HOW DO I SAY IT?? THEY'RE LIKE ARISTOCRATS!
THAT'S BECAUSE THEY ARE ARISTOCRATS.
TRUE ONES.
SO!
BE HUMBLE SO THAT THEY LOVE YOU.
TRY TO BECOME THEIR MASCOT!
UH-HUH!
SKRTCH SKRTCH
GUIDELINES FOR GUARDIANS... YUP.
BECOME THEIR MASCOT.
DO YOUR BEST TO HAVE EVERYONE IN THE NIGHT CLASS LIKE YOU.
AS YOU KNOW...
SKRTCH SKRTCH
ZERO, YOU TOO.
...
...EVENTUALLY YOU'LL BE JOINING TH--
GRIB
GASP GASP
...
WHAT ARE YOU SAYING?!
GRIB GRIB
NOT PAYING ATTENTION
BY THE WAY, YOU USED TO GO ON PATROL, RIGHT, HEADMASTER?
GRIB GRIB GRIB

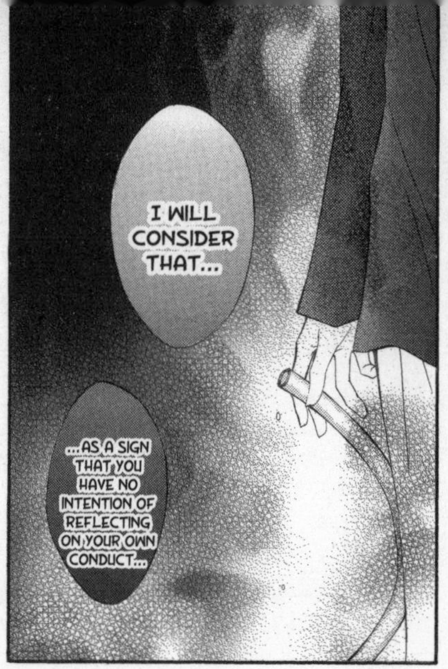

THE EVE BEFORE THE GUARDIANS MADE THEIR DEBUT

THE BUCKET AND KANAME-SAMA

KANAME-SAMA AND...

THIS GIRL WILL APPEAR IN VOLUME 3. ↑

THE BUCKET AND KANAME-SAMA

VAMPIRES COVERED IN BLOOD ARE PROHIBITED FROM ENTERING THIS PAGE!!

WHAT AM I TO YOU... (EIGHTH NIGHT)

BONUS STORY: I MUST'VE BEEN BORN UNDER THE "VICTIM OF CIRCUMSTANCES" STAR.../END

DAMN! HE BIT HER!
AIDO!
KAIN...
...I CONSIDER THAT YOU BROKE THE RULES TOO BECAUSE YOU WERE WITH AIDO BUT YOU DIDN'T STOP HIM.
ONE WEEK'S SUSPEN-SION.
※NIGHT CLASS RULES: DRINKING BLOOD ON CAMPUS IS FORBIDDEN.
What happened after first night.
VICTIM OF CIRCUMSTANCES
(ALSO CALLED ENTANGLEMENT)
...
GANG LEADER ...
WELL, THINGS ARE ALWAYS LIKE THIS.
Third night: On the roof, right before the brawl begins.
YOU HAVE NO RIGHT TO BREATHE THE SAME AIR AS KANAME-SAMA!
IT DOESN'T ONLY HAPPEN WITH HANABUSA.
I'LL PUT THUMB-TACKS IN YOUR SHOES NEXT TIME. BE PRE-PARED!
HEY.
KIRYU, RUKA...
...DON'T START FIGHTING...
Akatsuki Kain

IDOL?!
IT SOUNDS LIKE YOU'RE AN IDIOT--THAT'S ALL RIGHT WITH YOU?
IF YOU'RE HAPPY WITH IT, IT'S FINE BY ME.
WHAT ABOUT THAT GUY NEXT TO HIM?
THE GIRLS PONDER.
WELL, HE LOOKS WILDER THAN IDOL, SO...
CAN WE CALL YOU "WILD"?! ♡
AS A VICTIM OF CIRCUMSTANCES, AKATSUKI KAIN RECEIVED A NICKNAME TOO.
WILD! ♡♡
WELL...
...THINGS USUALLY GO LIKE THIS.
YOU SEE...
...HANABUSA AND I ARE COUSINS, AND WE ARE ROOMMATES.
WE TEND TO DO THINGS TOGETHER A LOT.
I WANT TO LIVE ON THE MOON...
SO THE MOMENT I LOOK THE OTHER WAY...
CHOMP

BUT THERE ARE LOTS OF CUTE GIRLS...
...SO THIS IS GOING TO BE A FUN NEW TERM!
KYA
AH-!!
WOW...
...AIDO'S LIKE AN IDOL...
TWITCH
Yuki, a new student.
ALTHOUGH HE'S A VAMPIRE...
YES...
AIDO... IDOL...
IDOL... AIDO...
?!
AIDO?
IDOL!
CAN WE CALL YOU "IDOL"?!
OF COURSE!
HEY. HANABUSA...
AKATSUKI, THIS IS THE FIRST TIME I'VE BEEN GIVEN A NICKNAME!
IDOLLLL!
PEEK
PEEK

THE EVENING BEFORE THE DAY CLASS ENTRANCE CEREMONY (THREE MONTHS AGO).
TO ALL NEW STUDENTS OF THE DAY CLASS...
...THANK YOU FOR COMING TO THE "FRIENDSHIP EVENING."
YAWN
FRIENDSHIP EVENING
SPONSORED BY HEADMASTER CROSS
I'M HANABUSA AIDO, REPRESENTING THE NIGHT CLASS.
THOUGH TO TELL THE TRUTH, THE NIGHT CLASS AND THE DAY CLASS DON'T HAVE A CHANCE OF MEETING TOO OFTEN...
VAMPIRE KNIGHT
BONUS STORY: I MUST'VE BEEN BORN UNDER THE "VICTIM OF CIRCUMSTANCES" STAR...
...
SO IT IS TRUE THAT EVERYONE IN THE NIGHT CLASS IS BEAUTIFUL AND ELITE!

THERE, STEP BACK! STEP BACK!
WE DO NEED THE DISCIPLINARY COMMITTEE.
THEY HELP KEEP THINGS PLEASANT.
HEH
YOU'RE RIGHT.
THANK YOU...
...MISS DISCIPLINARY COMMITTEE.
NO PROBLEM!
THE DAILY DUTIES OF THE GUARDIANS START HERE...
SOMETIMES THERE ARE LAZY DAYS TOO/END

LADIES...
...YOU SHOULD STOP MAKING A FUSS.
OTHER-WISE...
...I'M AFRAID YOU'LL GET HURT.
SILENCE
TWEEEET!
EVERY-BODY, CALM DOWN!

ARE YOU ALL RIGHT?
...
YES.
BAD AURA
DON'T YOU DARE TOUCH KANAME-SAMA!
!
RUKA.

KYAAH
HUH?
KYAAH
WHAT'S GOING ON?!
THE DISCIPLINARY COMMITTEE ISN'T HERE TODAY?
KYAAH
KYAAH!
DOMP
SLUMP
SHUFF
!
STEP BACK!
YOU BRATS HAVE NO CLASS AT ALL!
...

BAM
HA...
KREEEE
KYAAHH
TMP
TMP
TMP

ZERO, THIS ISN'T GOOD.
THE NIGHT CLASS STUDENTS WILL BE LEAVING THEIR DORM SOON.
NO TALKING!
JOLT
VUP
KIRYU!
TMP
TMP
TMP
WOW, HE'S BOLD.
KLNK
IT'S PAD-LOCKED.
WHEN DID HE... ?
HAH!
IF YOU WANT TO LEAVE, YOU HAVE TO FINISH ALL YOUR WORK FIRST.
KEY
HE'S LOST IT...
TODAY I WILL MAKE YOU BE SERIOUS STUDENTS, JUST LIKE HOW MEMBERS OF THE DISCIPLINARY COMMITTEE SHOULD ACT!
IT'S THE HEADMASTER'S FAULT FOR PUTTING STUDENTS LIKE YOU ON THE DISCIPLINARY COMMITTEE!
HA HA HA HA HA HA HA HA HA

I CAN'T TAKE IT ANYMORE! CROSS! KIRYU!
YOU'VE GOT SUPPLEMENTARY CLASSES UNTIL LATE!
I DON'T CARE ABOUT YOUR DISCIPLINARY COMMITTEE DUTIES!
DOOM
...
...
OPEN YOUR TEXTBOOKS.
I WON'T LET YOU LEAVE UNTIL YOU'VE DONE EVERYTHING WE'VE COVERED IN CLASS.
WHAT SHOULD WE DO, ZERO?
WE'VE GOT TO STAY HERE FOR NOW.
IT IS OUR FAULT WE'RE HERE.
WELL... YES... YOU'RE RIGHT.
YEAH ...
KYAAH
KYAAH

VI

Recently I've received comments about the manga I drew before *Vampire Knight*. There are people who have been reading my manga since my very first work... I'm a very fortunate person. (So wh-what do you think? Has my manga matured a little?)

To those who are solely devoted to vampires, and to those who have eaten vegetables from Hino's other fields, please keep on reading! ♡

Thank you for your letters. Reading them cheers me up. It's difficult for me to reply, but I'll do my best to pay you back with my work! Thank you so much...!!

◆

In volumes 1 and 2, perhaps Zero was more like the heroine than Yuki? From now on I plan to have Yuki do her best, like a heroine should. In the next volume, I'm planning on writing these sidebars based on a theme. We should be able to meet again, a bit sooner next time...!

See you!!
Matsuri Hino

YOU'RE ...
...NOT AFRAID OF ME?
CHOMF
...
SHNRB
SWUFF
...
SWUFF
YOU'RE A STRANGE ONE...
...JUST LIKE ME.

HER PERSON-ALITY...
...IS THE PROBLEM.
TUG
SHIRR
WELL, SHE LIKES YOU.
YOU'RE WHITE LILY'S BOY-FRIEND.
NUDGE
NUDGE
I NURSED HER WHEN SHE WAS A FOAL...
CHOMP
SHIRR
OKAY, OKAY, YOU WANT TO BE BRUSHED, RIGHT?
DON'T EAT MY HAIR!
I'LL GO BALD!
SHE'S IN A GOOD MOOD NOW.
I GUESS SHE'LL BE OKAY FOR TOMORROW'S RIDING LESSONS.
...
YOU HAVEN'T BEEN HERE IN A WHILE.
DID SOME-THING HAPPEN?

WAIT FOR ME, YORI!
TMP TMP TMP
WATCH OUT OR YOU'LL STUMBLE.
BONK
OUCH!
I CAN'T BELIEVE YOU GOT CAUGHT IN THE DOOR...
YUKI...
SHIRRT
SHUP
I'M GLAD YOU'RE HERE.
WHITE LILY IS IN A BAD MOOD TODAY.
RWL
RWL

WHY'D YOU SIGH LIKE THAT?
I-I DIDN'T FORGET MY DUTIES!
OH REALLY?
WAIT, ZERO!
ONLY THE HEADMASTER, WHO IS MY ADOPTED FATHER, AND WE DISCIPLINARY COMMITTEE MEMBERS...
...KNOW THAT EVERYONE IN THE NIGHT CLASS IS A VAMPIRE.
THE DISCIPLINARY COMMITTEE IS HERE TO KEEP PEACE IN THE SCHOOL, DAY AND NIGHT...
...SO THAT NO ONE FINDS OUT THE SECRET.
WE ARE ACTUALLY THE SCHOOL GUARDIANS.
YUKI...
...WAKE UP.
I JUST GOT INTO BED...
BUT TODAY'S BREAK-FAST...
...IS YOUR FAVORITE-- THE GINGER STIR-FRY SET.
YOU'LL MISS OUT.
VUMP

GOOD NIGHT...
...MISS DISCIPLINARY COMMITTEE.
THERE IS A POWER IN HIS SMILE...
...A POWER THAT ALMOST PULLS ME IN...
KREEE
KLNK
PHOO
PHEW!
AH!

I SEE. THAT'S GOOD.
UM... KANAME...
HOW WAS YOUR NIGHT, KANAME?
UM...
I'D LIKE TO SAY THAT...
I WANT TO HAVE A CASUAL CHAT WITH HIM...
GOOD NIGHT... ...KANAME.
BUT I ALWAYS GET TOO NERVOUS.

IT'S TIME FOR THE CROSS ACADEMY NIGHT CLASS...
...TO RETURN TO THEIR DORM.
WELCOME BACK, NIGHT CLASS.
YUKI CROSS, DAY CLASS, DISCIPLINARY COMMITTEE MEMBER
ZERO KIRYU, DAY CLASS, DISCIPLINARY COMMITTEE MEMBER
WE'RE BACK.
ANYTHING UNUSUAL HAPPEN?
NO, NOT TONIGHT.
IT WAS A QUIET EVENING.

KREEE
DONG
VAMPIRE KNIGHT
BONUS STORY:
SOMETIMES THERE ARE LAZY DAYS TOO

I...

...WILL NOT REGRET MY DECISION.

NINTH NIGHT/END

GRIP
YUKI...

SHFF
I WON'T...
...RUN AWAY ANY-MORE...
...SO...
...DON'T CRY.

ZERO...
...I REALLY THOUGHT YOU WERE GOING TO DIE.

ZERO.
THAT WOMAN...
...APPARENTLY SHE'S STILL ALIVE.
WHAT WOMAN?

BUT YOU'LL GET HURT IF YOU TREAT HIM GENTLY.
HE WON'T STOP UNLESS YOU PUT A BULLET IN HIM.
IT'S BETTER FOR HIM THAT WAY.
DAMN THIS IS HEAVY.
AFTER THAT... IT'S UP TO YOU.
THIS MAN...
THEN YOU SHOT ZERO IN THE POOL BECAUSE...
IF I MEANT TO KILL HIM, ONE BULLET WOULD'VE BEEN ENOUGH.
YOU THINK I'D MISS AT THAT DISTANCE?! DON'T MAKE ME LAUGH.
HEY, SEND THIS LUGGAGE TO ME LATER.
I'M DONE HERE. I HAVE MY NEXT ASSIGNMENT, SO I'VE GOT TO HURRY.
TUNK
UM...
RIGHT.
SEE YOU.
THE NEXT TIME WE MEET, YOU MIGHT BE ON MY LIST TOO...

DON'T RUN AWAY...
...ZERO.
HEY. LITTLE GIRL.
IF HE STARTS GOING BERSERK AGAIN, YOU STOP HIM.
"LITTLE GIRL"?!
WH-WHAT IS IT?

"I'LL MAKE SURE YOU DON'T REGRET LOSING YOUR EYE TO SAVE MY LIFE."
THAT DAY, YOU YOURSELF...
...MADE THAT VOW TO ME.
WATCHING YOU RIGHT NOW MADE ME WANT TO KILL YOU FOR REAL.
I HAVE NO INTENTION OF SAVING A KID WHO ONLY WANTS TO TAKE THE EASY WAY OUT.
STRUGGLE UNTIL YOU CAN'T STRUGGLE ANYMORE.
JUST NOW, YOU DECIDED TO LIVE YOUR LIFE COVERED IN BLOOD.

...
YOU DECIDED TO STOP WAITING FOR ME TO KILL YOU?
DAMN IT!
DON'T YOU REMEMBER?!

STOP! ZERO!!
BLAM BLAM

BAM
KLIK
...

ZERO?!
...
KRRK
CROSS!
BAM
Prohibited
...
I'M A FOOL!
TMP
I SHOULDN'T HAVE LEFT ZERO ALONE...
No Entr
HUFF

EVEN THOUGH THAT BULLET DIDN'T HIT YOU, A VAMPIRE GUN CAN DO GREAT DAMAGE.
ALTHOUGH VAMPIRES HEAL QUICKLY, IT WILL STILL TAKE QUITE SOME TIME...
...UNLESS YOU DRINK THE BLOOD FROM A LIVING PERSON...
P-TOOOM
HE'S NOT COMING.
HE DOESN'T WANT TO COME?

IF YOU SHOW THAT MAN YOU'RE ALL RIGHT...
...HE'LL HAVE NO REASON TO KILL YOU.
WHY DO YOU HAVE ALL THE WINDOWS CLOSED?
TUNK
SHFF
HOW'S...
...YOUR RIGHT SHOULDER?
HUH?

IT'S SO THAT I WON'T LOSE...
...MY GIRL.
ZERO, YOU SHOULD COME TO SCHOOL.
PLEASE...
COME TO SCHOOL.

YET YOU WON'T DO ANYTHING, JUST LIKE A PROPER HONOR STUDENT.
WHY IS THAT?
WHY WON'T YOU TEAR ZERO TO SHREDS?
SHAA
SHINK

V

Some of the letters I receive from my readers say, "I wouldn't mind having my blood drunk by Zero (or Kaname)."♡ I think it's fun.♡ Reading those letters made me seriously imagine who I would prefer to bite me. But...the beast in me (smile) did not allow me to.

I need my blood! I've got anemia... I'm an anemic brown bear...!! So I can't donate blood. I'm sorry...

Since I'm talking about beasts... Regarding the animal zodiacs, we often say in our workplace that Yuki is a boar and Zero is a dog. (smile)

...
GOOD-NIGHT...
...YUKI.
I WILL NOT REGRET WHAT I MADE ZERO DO.
GOOD-NIGHT...
...KANAME.
NEVER.
BUT WHY...
...DOES MY HEART ACHE SO?

IN TEN YEARS...
...THAT'S THE ONLY THING THAT HAS CHANGED.

KANAME ...?
I WONDER WHEN...
...YOU STOPPED TELLING ME EVERYTHING, YUKI.

HE REALIZES WHAT'S HAPPENED...
DON'T LOOK.
DON'T LOOK AT MY NECK!

YOUR HAIR... IS WET...
SUFF
WHAT WERE YOU WASHING AWAY?
OH!
...
OF COURSE HE KNOWS...

YUKI...
...WHERE HAVE YOU BEEN?
JOLT
UM...
THE NIGHT CLASS LESSONS...
THEY'VE FINISHED.
I MADE EVERYONE GO HOME.
I NEED TO TALK TO THE HEAD-MASTER.
IS HE IN HIS PRIVATE LIVING AREA?
NO.
I SEE.
TAK

IT'S A SIN TO KEEP A VAMPIRE ALIVE...
...BY OFFERING MY OWN BLOOD AS BAIT.
HUFF
WE ARE DOING SOMETHING THAT IS FORBIDDEN...
NO ONE MUST FIND OUT ABOUT THIS.

BOTH OF US...
NOTHING HAS CHANGED.
ZERO, PLEASE COME TO SCHOOL TOMORROW.
PROMISE ME.
SWAY
...UNDER-STAND, BUT NEITHER OF US WILL SAY IT.

IF YOU HAVEN'T COMPLETELY LOST YOUR SANITY...
...I WON'T LET YOU DIE.
HATE VAMPIRES, HATE ME...
AT LEAST THAT MEANS YOU HAVEN'T GIVEN UP!
HOW CAN I HATE YOU?
!
ARE YOU... ALL RIGHT?
?
OH.
YEAH, I'M OKAY. I'M NOT ANEMIC-- I'M FINE AS USUAL...
I CAN GO TO SCHOOL TOMORROW TOO.

YOU KNOW IT TOO...
...THIS IS JUST LIKE THE BLOOD TABLETS. IT'S ONLY A TEMPORARY MEASURE.
PLEASE, BEFORE I ACQUIRE A TASTE FOR YOUR BLOOD...
YOU ASK ME TO GIVE UP ON YOU.
IT'S CRUEL OF YOU TO ASK THAT OF ME...
BUT I WILL KEEP MY PROMISE.
I TOLD YOU THAT I WOULD STOP YOU.
EVEN IF YOU HATE ME, ZERO...
I WILL TAME THAT BEAST IN YOU...
...AS MANY TIMES AS NECESSARY.

...
I'M SUCH...
...A WRETCHED BEING.
EVEN IF I LOATHE VAMPIRES...
...EVEN IF I DON'T WANT TO HURT ANYONE...
...I CAN'T STOP MYSELF FROM LUSTING FOR BLOOD.
JUST GIVE UP ON ME...

TOMP
HUFF
HUFF
ZERO...
...ARE YOU ALL RIGHT?

A VAMPIRE...
...IS GOING TO...
...EAT ME...
I'M SCARED...
GULK
I'M AFRAID?
THEN WHAT ABOUT ZERO?
SHFF

GULK
I'M...
...SCARED...
HUFF
GRIP

VAMPIRE
KNIGHT
NINTH NIGHT: CHOICES MADE

I DIDN'T THINK YOU'D AGREE TO COME HERE, CROSS.
HOW IS KIRYU'S SON DOING?
HAS HE NOW BECOME TOO MUCH FOR YOU TO HANDLE?
OF COURSE NOT...
ZERO HASN'T LOST HIS SANITY YET.
I WILL WAIT FOR A REPORT ABOUT THE TRUTH OF THAT.
I SENT YAGARI TO YOUR SCHOOL...
HE WILL GET RID OF KIRYU'S SON IF HE DECIDES HE'S BECOME DANGEROUS.
THERE'S NOTHING THAT THE HUNTER SOCIETY NEEDS TO WORRY ABOUT...
IT'S REGRETTABLE YOU'RE SUSPICIOUS ABOUT THE PEACE AT CROSS ACADEMY...
TMP

...THE MOST FORBIDDEN ACT OF ALL...
EIGHTH NIGHT/END

I'M SORRY...
HUFF
WE'LL DO...

DRINK MY BLOOD, ZERO...
...
PLEASE... DON'T...
I WON'T BE ABLE TO FORGIVE MYSELF...
YES...
YOU'LL FEEL BETTER...
...EVEN IF ONLY FOR A LITTLE WHILE...
I KNOW.

WHAT...
...ARE YOU SAYING?
PUSH
THIS IS THE BEST WAY...
...ZERO.
SHOON

YUKI...
...IS A KIND GIRL...
I REALIZE NOW THAT THIS IS THE ONLY THING I CAN DO FOR YOU.

KREEEAK
THE NEXT CLASS IS STARTING. YOU'RE NOT COMING BACK TO THE CLASS-ROOM?
POP
I'M NOT INTERESTED IN THAT OLD MAN'S MACROECO-NOMICS.
BY THE WAY...
...YUKI WENT OFF SOME-WHERE.
IS SOME-THING BOTHERING HER?
POK
KANAME ?

VUNK
NO ONE WILL NOTICE US IN HERE...
DRIP
LET'S CONTINUE...
WHERE WE LEFT OFF LAST NIGHT...
SHUFF

ZERO...
WHY WON'T YOU LOOK AT ME?
LET ME IN.
CHAK
YUKI?

...TRYING TO GIVE UP ON EVERYTHING!
YOU'RE GIVING UP ON YOURSELF!
YOU GAVE ME THAT GUN...
...SO DON'T RUN AWAY FROM ME!

EVEN WHEN HER NECK WAS SMASHED, SHE KEPT BARING HER FANGS UNTIL THE MOMENT SHE DIED...
...AND I BECAME AFRAID OF VAMPIRES FOR THE FIRST TIME.
MY MASTER TAUGHT ME THINGS THROUGH HIS ACTIONS.
SO IF HE'S GOING TO KILL ME, I...
...
NO!
ZERO, YOU'RE JUST...

THAT MAN...
...TOOK CARE OF ME AND MY YOUNGER BROTHER.
HE WAS MY GUARDIAN AND MY TEACHER WHEN MY PARENTS WEREN'T AT HOME.
BACK THEN I SAW A LEVEL E VAMPIRE FOR THE FIRST TIME...
GRIP
THE DOCTOR AT OUR ELEMENTARY SCHOOL...
...WAS A REALLY NICE, BEAUTIFUL WOMAN.
BUT SHE WAS A FORMER HUMAN WHO HAD RUN AWAY FROM AN ARISTOCRAT.
ONE DAY SHE SUDDENLY TRANSFORMED INTO A FEROCIOUS VAMPIRE RIGHT IN FRONT OF US.
I BLOCKED MY MASTER'S WAY...
...PLEADING WITH HIM THAT SHE WAS A GOOD PERSON...
HE LOST AN EYE DUE TO MY IGNORANCE.

I'M FINE.
GO HOME, YUKI.
WAIT, ZERO!
HUH?
WHY ARE YOU STAYING HERE...
TUG
...JUST BECAUSE THAT MAN TOLD YOU TO?

...THERE'S NOTHING...
...A GOOD LITTLE GIRL LIKE YOU CAN DO.
IF YOU STILL WANT TO SEE HIM...
...GO.
HE'S IN THE GUEST ROOM OF THE HEADMASTER'S PRIVATE LIVING AREA.

KR EEK
CHAK
YOU WAITED ALL THIS TIME?
I THOUGHT YOU'D GO OFF TO FIND ZERO.
YOU SAID ZERO WAS OKAY...
I WAS AFRAID THE NIGHT CLASS WOULD TEAR YOU TO SHREDS.
I DON'T WANT TO PRETEND TO OVERLOOK THINGS LIKE THAT...
...AS A GUARDIAN.
FEH
...
HOW GOOD OF YOU.
HOW-EVER...

RELAX.
TODAY I AM AN OFFICIAL TEACHER...
...WITH A TEACHING CERTIFI-CATE.
I HEARD THAT YOU WERE SOMEWHERE FAR AWAY, BUT YOU'VE RETURNED?
YOU'VE COME BACK TO CHECK OUT THE NIGHT CLASS?
OR IS THERE A VAMPIRE AMONG US WHO YOU WANT TO KILL...
...TEACHER?
SHIFF
HELLO, KANAME KURAN.
UNFORTUNATELY MY EXECUTION LIST IS EMPTY RIGHT NOW.
IF YOU FALL ASLEEP BECAUSE MY LECTURE IS BORING, I CAN ADD YOU TO THE LIST, YOU KNOW?
HEH...
I'LL BE CAREFUL...
POK
...TEACHER.

TAK
TAK
TAK
BAM
I'M TOGA YAGARI. I'LL BE YOUR TEMPORARY LECTURER FOR THIS ETHICS CLASS.
NICE TO MEET YOU, VAMPIRES...
"YAGARI"?
HE HAS THE SAME NAME AS THE MAN WHO'S THE NO. 1 VAMPIRE HUNTER RIGHT NOW...
SO IT WAS YOU SHOOTING LAST NIGHT...

...A TEMPORARY LECTURER OF ETHICS FOR THE NIGHT CLASS.
YOU'RE... A LECTURER?
DO YOUR OWN JOB.
SLAM
KLIK

WHAT HAPPENED TO ZERO?
GRAB
HE'S NOT AT SCHOOL OR THE DORM. THE HEADMASTER ISN'T AROUND EITHER...
WHAT DID YOU DO TO HIM?!
WE QUARAN-TINED HIM, OF COURSE.
QUARAN-TINED...?
HE'S TO THE POINT WHERE HE'LL ATTACK AT ANY TIME.
WE QUARANTINED HIM SO THAT THERE WON'T BE ANY VICTIMS UNTIL I SETTLE THINGS.
BUT ZERO IS SAFE FOR NOW, RIGHT?
WHERE IS HE?!
LET ME GO! I'VE GOT WORK TO DO!
THAT RETIRED TWIT TOLD ME I WOULDN'T BE ABLE TO STAY HERE UNLESS I DID SOMETHING!
HE FORCED ME TO BECOME...

HIS WORDS ECHO IN MY HEAD.
IT'S ALL RIGHT.
ZERO DIDN'T COME TO SCHOOL.

YUKI...
YOU'VE HAD SOMETHING ON YOUR MIND RECENTLY.
IS THERE ANYTHING I CAN DO TO HELP?
I CAN'T...
...DO ANYTHING EITHER.
ZERO...
YUKI...
IT'S ALL RIGHT.

ZERO CAN'T TOLERATE BLOOD TABLETS...
...SO HIS BODY WILL CONTINUE TO LUST FOR BLOOD...
AND HIS MIND IS BEING EATEN AWAY...
IF THINGS CONTINUE LIKE THIS, ZERO WILL...
YUKI?
OH!
I WOKE YOU UP. I'M SORRY...

ZERO WAS ABOUT TO ATTACK YOU...
...YET YOU CONSIDER ME AS YOUR ENEMY.
LET ME TAKE CARE OF THINGS...
...YOU GO HOME, YUKI.
THEY WENT TO THE HEAD-MASTER'S ROOM...
I WAS THE ONE WHO WAS SHUT OUT.
THE HEADMASTER SAID THERE'S NOTHING TO WORRY ABOUT...
...BUT THAT MAN SAID HE'D KILL ZERO...

IV

↓(continued)
But there are lots of things that degrade Kaname-sama. I would never be able to reveal them, because it would ruin his image. (← What did you try to make him do, Hino...?)

◆

The other day, my editor complimented me, saying that Zero's hand gestures look great and that Kaname's hand gestures look sexy. ♡I'm happy!♡ But there is something I couldn't say then: To my editor and to all my readers... I apologize for ruining your fantasies... The model for those hands is...

...me! My desperate hands... The hands whose gestures were called lewd when I was small... (I changed my hands into male versions...)
I'm sorry. Zero. Kaname-tama. (Did I ruin their image?)

HEY, PUT THAT THING AWAY!
I DROPPED BY BECAUSE I WAS WORRIED, AND THIS IS WHAT I FIND!
HOW MUCH LONGER ARE YOU GOING TO KEEP A GIRL IN COLD WATER?!
YOU MUST BE FREEZING. HERE, GRAB MY HANDS.
...
DRIP
VUSH
VUSH
WHO...
...ARE YOU?

YUKI.
IT'S ALL RIGHT.
PUSH
YOU TOOK THINGS TOO FAR!
THIS IS EXACTLY WHY I HATE VAMPIRE HUNTERS!!

YOU'RE...
...THE ADOPTED DAUGHTER OF THAT RETIRED TWIT?
I DON'T KNOW WHAT YOUR RELATION-SHIP WITH ZERO IS...
I WON'T LET YOU KILL HIM!
...BUT WHETHER ZERO LIVES OR DIES IS NOT FOR YOU TO DECIDE!
ARE YOU SAYING HE ISN'T A LEVEL E YET?

...
ZERO...
EVEN IF YOU ARE HUNGERING FOR BLOOD...
...DO YOU STILL HAVE A REASON TO BRACE YOURSELF FOR THIS?
SWFF
CHAK

SPLASH
ZERO!
...
B-BMP
AAH!
EVEN IF THE BULLET ONLY WHIZZED BY YOU, IT MUST HURT LIKE HELL.
A SPELL WAS PUT ON THAT BULLET TO KILL VAMPIRES.

VAMPIRES CAN ONLY EVER BE OUR ENEMY.

VAMPIRE KNIGHT
EIGHTH NIGHT: THE FORBIDDEN ACT
WHY DO VAMPIRES HURT HUMANS?
BECAUSE THEY ARE PITIFUL BEINGS WHO LIVE ONLY BY INSTINCT.
THAT'S WHY WE HUNT THEM.
VAMPIRE HUNTERS LIKE ME AND THE KIRYU FAMILY EXIST FOR THAT PURPOSE.
ZERO...
...YOU DO UNDERSTAND NOW?

IT WAS MY FAULT...
...YOUR EYE...
I'M SORRY, MASTER.
YOU TOLD ME TO RUN AWAY...
...BUT I CAME BACK.
...
HUH?
ARE YOU GONNA MAKE ME REGRET THAT I RISKED MY LIFE TO PROTECT YOU?
SHEESH.
DAMN BRAT.
GRIP
I DIDN'T SAVE YOU SO THAT YOU COULD MAKE A FACE LIKE THAT.
MASTER...

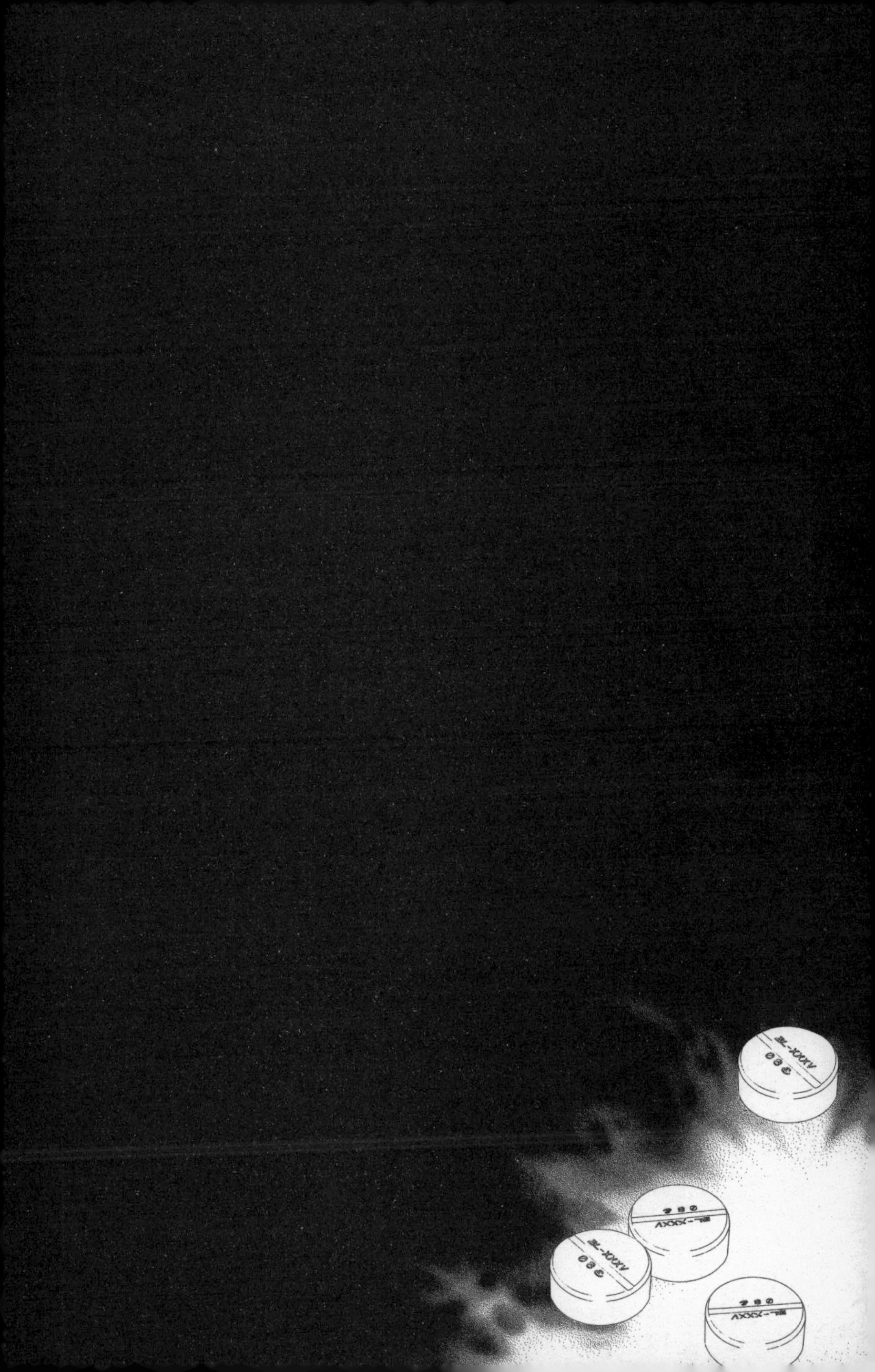

CURSE ME WITH YOUR LAST BREATH AND DIE...
...VAMPIRE.
MAS...
...TER...
?!
SEVENTH NIGHT/END

I NEVER THOUGHT I'D BE KILLING MY DEAR STUDENT WITH THIS GUN.

SPLOSH
WHUEEE
PTOOM

I HAVE TO STOP HIM!

B-DMP
YOU CAN'T ACT AS IF NOTHING HAS CHANGED.
HAAH
I HAVE TO STOP HIM.
TMP
VLUGGG

ZERO...

ZERO ?!
WHAT IS IT ?
ARE YOU ALL RIGHT ?
URGH...
YUKI...
VAMPIRES WHO USED TO BE HUMAN...
...SOMETIMES...

...CAN'T TOLERATE BLOOD TABLETS.
AFTER I ATTACKED YOU...
...I TOOK THEM EVERY NIGHT...
...BUT...
...THEY ALWAYS MADE ME FEEL SICK...
!
GRIP
THE BLOOD TABLETS HAVEN'T HELPED HIM SINCE THEN?
YOU'RE HURTING ME...
...ZERO.
THEN ZERO IS...

HUFF
MMM ...
I WILL STOP YOU, ZERO.
ZERO...
...
YOU HEARD IT TOO?
THE SOUND OF YOUR BLOOD BEING SUCKED IN BY ME.

TOK
HE TOOK AWAY PHYSICAL PAIN... VAMPIRES HAVE THIS POWER TOO.
BLOOD TABLETS?
KLAK
IS THIS ZERO'S?

THE VICE PRESIDENT TOOK THE TROUBLE OF SETTING THINGS UP FOR YOU...
YOU DON'T SEEM TOO CONCERNED ...
HEH
YUKI...
...WILL EVENTUALLY COME TO ME...
I DIDN'T LIKE THAT ATMOSPHERE ...
ZERO PROBABLY FELT THAT WAY TOO.
IT'S NOT HURTING ANYMORE! THAT MEANS...
ZERO!
BLUSH

HUFFF
VRK
SHK
SHK
HERE.
SHIKI? DRINK THIS INSTEAD.
I HAVE NO INTENTION OF SERVING MYSELF TO YOU.
THIS IS BORING TO DRINK.
UHHHHHH...
TOO BAD.
GRIP
SHOULD YOU HAVE LET HER GO LIKE THAT?
IT'S ALL RIGHT...
...FOR NOW...

HUH ?
ZERO ?!
ZERO!
OOPS.
THEY PROBABLY FOUND IT GROSS...
HUH?
VUMP

OH...
...YOU CUT ME.
OOPS.
SORRY.
KRSS
DON'T WASTE IT...
YOU CUT ME ON PURPOSE, DIDN'T YOU...
...SHIKI ?
HMM?

HEE HEE
HA HA HA
SIGH
...
...
THIS ATMOSPHERE IS...
KANAME.
I'M LEAVING NOW.
GRIN GRIN
WHAT A HUGE CAKE... YOU'RE EATING IT BY YOURSELF?
THIS IS FOR EVERYONE.
YOU WANT TO CUT IT, SHIKI?
OF COURSE.
HOLD THE CAKE FOR ME, ICHIJO.

THEY'RE LIKE KNIGHTS WHO SECRETLY PROTECT PEOPLE...
STOP JOKING AROUND! YOU GIVE ME THE CREEPS.
THEY CALL IT THEIR DUTY...
...BUT THEY SIMPLY ENJOY HUNTING.
WE VAMPIRE HUNTERS...
...KILL VAMPIRES.
BUT IT IS FORBIDDEN TO KILL THEM WITHOUT REASON!
WHY ARE YOU HERE ANYWAY?
TMP
I DIDN'T COME TO SEE YOU. I'M HERE TO SEE ZERO.
I MADE A SERIOUS VOW WITH HIM.
A VOW, HUH.
BE NICE TO HIM, LIKE YOU USED TO.

IT MAY HAVE BEEN A MISTAKE TO LEAVE HIM IN YOUR CARE.
WHAT ARE YOU SAYING?
YOU HAD NO OTHER CHOICE.
I HAVEN'T SEEN HIM...
...FOR FOUR YEARS.
I DIDN'T THINK I'D BE ABLE TO SEE HIM AGAIN.
TODAY...
...A LEVEL E WANDERED INTO TOWN.
OH REALLY?
DID YOU DO YOUR "WORK"?
DON'T PRETEND YOU DON'T KNOW.
THEY TURNED IT TO ASHES FIRST.
THE NIGHT CLASS MUST HAVE SNATCHED IT.
THEY'RE THE ONLY ARISTOCRATS WHO CAN DO ANYTHING AROUND HERE.
HA HA HA!
WELL, THERE IS A SCHOOL RULE FORBIDDING THE NIGHT CLASS TO LEAVE SCHOOL GROUNDS WITHOUT PERMISSION.
THEY WON'T FOLLOW SUCH RULES!
WELL! I WONDER WHO IT WAS? SAVING OUR TOWN LIKE THAT!

WHAT A STERN FACE.
A REBELLIOUS PHASE?
KIRYU ISN'T A KID. HAVE IT IF YOU WANT.
I CAN HAVE ZERO?
NO, THE PHOTO.
I MADE SOME EXTRA PRINTS WHEN I WAS GOING THROUGH THEM.
THE GIRL IN THE PHOTO IS MY YUKI! ♡ SHE WOULD'VE BEEN ONE GRADE LOWER THAN ZERO, BUT SHE'S A DEPENDABLE DAUGHTER. ♡
MY CUTE YUKI! ♡
ON HER FIRST DAY OF HIGH SCHOOL, SHE HIT KIRYU TO GET HIM TO GO AGAIN. ♡
WHAT?!
"AGAIN"?!
YOU MEAN HE REPEATED A YEAR?!
IT'S ALL RIGHT. HE STANDS OUT IN THE CROWD, BUT HE'S DOING FINE.
YEAH.
KRK
HE REPEATED A YEAR IN JUNIOR HIGH.
WELL, I CAN SEE WHY HE HESITATED ABOUT GOING TO HIGH SCHOOL.
THE NIGHT CLASS ATTENDS THE SAME SCHOOL.
...HE'D HAVE TO SEE THE PUREBLOOD OFTEN.
I ASKED KIRYU...
...TO BE A THREAT TO THE NIGHT CLASS, WHICH CONSISTS OF PROBLEM STUDENTS.
WHAT HAPPENED TO YOUR SO-CALLED PACIFISM?
YOU DON'T TRUST THE NIGHT CLASS?
I DO.
BUT THEY'RE A HOT-HEADED BUNCH.

ARE YOU AFRAID?
EVER SINCE WE'VE KNOWN EACH OTHER I'VE BEEN A LITTLE AFRAID OF YOU...
...KANAME.
...EVEN NOW, I'M A BIT... AFRAID...
HEY!
DON'T FORGET, EVERYONE!
THIS IS MY BIRTHDAY PARTY!
YOU'VE ALL GOTTA CELEBRATE!
YUKI AND KIRYU ARE MY PRECIOUS GUESTS TOO!

BUT DON'T YOU FORGET...
...THE REASON WE'RE HERE.
WE'RE AT CROSS ACADEMY SOLELY BECAUSE...
...KANAME-SAMA, THE PUREBLOOD VAMPIRE, IS HERE.
KANAME IS A PURE-BLOOD VAMPIRE...
HE'S THE SAME KIND OF VAMPIRE WHO ATTACKED ZERO'S FAMILY...
YOU DIDN'T KNOW THAT ABOUT ME, YUKI?

I SAID SOMETHING I SHOULDN'T HAVE.
VUP
ZERO...
CROSSING
CHK
THAT WAS SCARY.
KIRYU POINTED THAT GUN AT KANAME-SAMA...
TEARING HIM INTO SHREDS RIGHT HERE WOULDN'T BE ENOUGH.
NOW, NOW, AIDO ...
...DON'T REALLY DO IT.
GRIP
YEAH...I WILL *TRY* NOT TO WHILE I'M AT THIS SCHOOL...
...I DON'T WANT TO HINDER THE HEADMASTER'S PACIFIST IDEOLOGY.

SHAA
PLIP
SEIREN...
...IT'S ALL RIGHT.

CROSSING
DANGER

THEN WHY DIDN'T YOU KILL HIM FIRST?
I'LL EASE YOUR PAIN...
PHOO
HUH?
K...
KANAME ...!
...YOU SYMPATHIZED WITH HIM?
PERHAPS, KIRYU...
HEH.

BUT IN THE OLD DAYS, HIDDEN FROM HIS-TORY...
...WHEN THE WAR BETWEEN VAMPIRES AND VAMPIRE HUNTERS WAS AT ITS PEAK...
...VAMPIRES TURNED MANY HUMANS INTO VAMPIRES TO USE IN BATTLE.
AND NOW THE ARISTOCRATS HAVE THE DUTY TO MANAGE THOSE SURVIVORS.
I DIDN'T KNOW THE NIGHT CLASS WAS DOING SUCH THINGS.
KANAME...
SOMETIMES WE HAVE TO KILL THEM OFF...
SHFF
IT IS THE VAMPIRE HUNTER'S DUTY TO KILL VAMPIRES.

KANA-ME...
...UM...
B-BMP
I'M SORRY ABOUT TODAY.
I DIDN'T THINK...
...YOU WOULD BE THERE WHEN THE HUNTING TOOK PLACE...
B-BMP
NO... IT WAS FINE.
BUT...
GRASP
...IT'S YOUR FAULT TOO, FOR WANDERING AROUND THERE.
B-BMP
SUFF
B-BMP
DID YOU INJURE YOUR ARM BECAUSE OF THAT VAMPIRE?
IT MUST HURT.
JOLT
NO, IT WAS BECAUSE I WAS CARE-LESS.
HUMANS SHOULD NEVER...
...BE TURNED INTO VAMPIRES.

I'M FINE.
YUKI.
TMPH
...OKAY...
SHF
?!
THIS IS THE SAFEST PLACE FOR YOU TO BE...

TMPH
...
TMP
YUKI...
...SIT BESIDE ME.
HUH?
...NO THANKS.
...
PEEK

YOU ORDERED ...
...THAT VAMPIRE TO BE...
YUKI.
WHY DIDN'T YOU INFORM THE HEAD-MASTER?
YOU'RE A MEMBER OF THE DISCIPLINARY COMMITTEE, YET WHEN ICHIJO INVITED YOU, YOU CAME HERE...
BUT!
...TO A DANGEROUS PLACE LIKE THIS.
I DIDN'T THINK IT WAS SOMETHING I SHOULD REPORT...
...AND I WANTED TO KNOW THE TRUTH FIRST-HAND.
FIRSTHAND, HUH...
YUKI, KIRYU...
...COME OVER HERE.

...UNDER MY ORDERS.
ZAA
KANAME-SAMA IS HERE...
IT'S KANAME-SAMA...
KANAME!
KANAME-SAMA IS ATTENDING THE SOIREE!
HOW UNUSUAL ...
ZAA

THAT IS WHY FORMER HUMANS ARE MANAGED BY THE ARISTOCRATS AND ABOVE.
M-MANAGED ...?
BUT ACCIDENTS DO OCCUR.
A MAD VAMPIRE MAY FLEE FROM AN ARISTO-CRAT...
...AND WANDER INTO HUMAN SOCIETY.
THERE WAS A REPORT THAT A LEVEL E VAMPIRE WOULD APPEAR IN TOWN TODAY.
ZAA
ICHIJO AND SHIKI HUNTED IT DOWN...

III

As you can see——

Kaname wears his uniform properly, but for his private clothes, he prefers ones that are pretty loose since they are more comfortable. I realized that when I was drawing him. (Is it okay for the mangaka to be like that?) Everything about him is supposed to have been predetermined, but there are unexpected discoveries. But!!! HE'S HARD TO DRAW! (↑ I wrote this with my left hand.)

His face and hair and form are—— And then at meetings my editor often jokes, "Kaname isn't someone of such low caliber that he would do that, right?" making me play the role of the comedic "straight man."

————Yes, Kaname is difficult to draw— even his conduct...!! I'm always full of curiosity when I draw Kaname (and other characters). I think, "I want to make them do this..."

↓ (continued)

THAT VAMPIRE USED TO BE HUMAN.
FILTHY THINGS.
...
AIDO!
YUKI, VAMPIRES ...
...ARE RULED BY A FEW PUREBLOODS AND A HANDFUL OF ARISTOCRATS.
EVERY STUDENT IN THE NIGHT CLASS IS AN ARISTOCRAT OR HIGHER...
TO USE A PYRAMID AS AN EXAMPLE ...
...FORMER HUMANS ARE LOWER THAN COMMON VAMPIRES.
<LEVEL A> PUREBLOODS
<LEVEL B> ARISTOCRATS
<LEVEL C> COMMON VAMPIRES
<LEVEL D> FORMER HUMANS
TO TELL THE TRUTH, THEY AREN'T TREATED VERY WELL.
THE VAMPIRE I KILLED ...
...WAS A LEVEL E VAMPIRE-- A VAMPIRE WHO'S FALLEN OUTSIDE THE PYRAMID.
<LEVEL C> COMMON VAMPIRES
<LEVEL D> FORMER HUMANS
<LEVEL E>
LEVEL E?

II

The Seventh Night is a story where lots of Night Class students will probably appear! So I drew seven characters for the chapter title page... This was the first time I drew so many people in one illustration, so it was difficult... I drew a coffin in the drawing. What secret lies in there? I like to put hidden meanings in my drawings. (Like the fang pendant on the Sixth Night chapter title page.)

Recently, my main drawing material for color illustrations is Copic markers. I own 222 colors, but this manga, I realized, uses only black, night colors, white, and blood colors--I haven't been able to use other colors. ◊ And I'm getting more blood colors. This is what it means to be drawing a vampire manga. ◊ (And the blood in my color illustrations--if it were all ketchup, it would be glutinous and funny.)

SMILE
SMILE
...
TONIGHT IS MY BIRTHDAY PARTY!
PLEASE ENJOY YOUR-SELVES!
THIS CORNER IS A WORLD OF ITS OWN.
HE'S TOO MUCH LIKE A HUMAN AND NOT ENOUGH LIKE A VAMPIRE...
JUST HIM, THOUGH.
SHE ASKS BECAUSE SHE THINKS IT'S EXPECTED OF HER.
H-HOW OLD ARE YOU?
HOW OLD IN HUMAN YEARS OR VAMPIRE YEARS?
DOIK
V...
...VAM-PIRE YEARS?
I'M EIGHTEEN. I'M A GROWNUP NOW! OH...
...I WANT YOU TO KISS ME FOR MY BIRTHDAY PRESENT, YUKI!
HUH?!
OH, THAT.
SHE'S NOT OKAY HERE AT ALL.
UM!
WE CAME HERE ON BUSINESS.
AS MEMBERS OF THE DISCIPLINARY COMMITTEE, WE WANT TO KNOW WHAT HAPPENED TODAY.
I CAN'T LOOK THE OTHER WAY. LEAVING SCHOOL GROUNDS WITH-OUT PERMISSION IS AGAINST SCHOOL RULES...
...AND... MORE-OVER...
...THAT VAMPIRE...

THIS IS WHAT VAMPIRES REALLY LOOK LIKE.
THIS WAY.
HERE THEY ARE, VICE PRESIDENT ICHIJO.
VEEN
WHAT ?
...NOTHING.
HE LOOKS THE SAME AS ALWAYS.
OH!
WELCOME, YUKI AND KIRYU!
SMILE
HUH ?!

LOOK WHO IS WITH THEM.
HANABUSA AIDO...AND AKATSUKI KAIN.
KANAME-SAMA'S RIGHT-HAND MEN...
THEY LOOK DIFFERENT THAN WHEN THEY'RE AT SCHOOL...
THE ONES WHO'VE CHANGED OUT OF THEIR UNIFORMS TONIGHT...

YEAH...
...ONLY BECAUSE ICHIJO ASKED US TO.
HE TOLD US TO GUARD YOU SO THAT OUR GUYS DON'T MESS WITH YOU.
UNFOR-TUNATELY, TONIGHT...
...ALMOST ALL OF THE NIGHT CLASS STUDENTS ...
...ARE HERE ON THE MOON DORM GROUNDS.
ZAA
HMPH, THEY CAME?
WHAT FOR ?
...
TING
I WOULDN'T IF I WERE YOU.
YOU'LL GO DOWN FIRST.

SHUP
KRK
DID YOU COME OUT TO WELCOME US...
...VAMPIRES?

WAIT, ZERO!
DON'T GO TO THE NIGHT CLASS DORM WHEN YOU'RE DYING TO SHOOT SOMEONE!
GRAB
I'M GLAD YOU'RE WORRIED ABOUT ME, ZERO...
...BUT I'M OKAY ON MY OWN. GO BACK.
...
IF YOU REALLY LOOKED LIKE YOU FELT OKAY...
...THEN I WOULDN'T HAVE TO BOTHER WITH THIS.
GEEZ YOU'RE MEAN.
WE'RE ON THE GROUNDS OF THE MOON DORM.
IT DOES HAVE ITS OWN ATMOSPHERE...
ESPE-CIALLY AT NIGHT...
SHAAAA

...
CALM DOWN!
BE MORE POSITIVE, KIRYU!
SHOOP SHOOP SHOOP
WHAT IS WITH THE HEAD-MASTER'S BOLD-NESS?
STIR-RING HIM UP...
KRAK
IS IT BECAUSE HE KNOWS EVERY-THING...
...ABOUT ZERO?
BASH BASH BASH
I WANT TO UNDER-STAND MORE...
...ABOUT ZERO...
...AND ABOUT VAMPIRES.
SO TONIGHT...
FLAP FLAP FLAP
KA-CHINK

BLOOD TABLETS.
...
ZIK
...
DON'T LOOK SO SHOCKED.
THIS IS GOING TO BECOME THE NORM FOR ME.
BUT ZERO MUST BE FEELING SHOCKED TOO...
YEAH...
WHY ARE YOU TWO LOOKING SO DOWN?
C'MON NOW.
REALLY!
THE TABLETS RESTRAIN THE URGE TO DRINK BLOOD...
...BUT IT'S ALSO JUST LIKE HAVING A MEAL! ♡

DID SOME-THING...
...HAPPEN WHILE YOU WERE IN TOWN?
YUKI, YOU WERE INJURED, RIGHT?
THE REASON WHY WE KILLED THAT VAMPIRE?
IF YOU WANT TO KNOW, COME TO THE BACK OF THE MOON DORM AT MIDNIGHT.
DON'T YOU WANT TO KNOW WHY?
I GOT HURT FROM ...
IS IT ALL RIGHT TO TELL...
...THE HEAD-MASTER?
ZERO HASN'T SAID ANYTHING ABOUT WHAT HAPPENED.
OH!
I'D FORGOT-TEN ALL ABOUT IT.
HERE, ZERO.
YOU'LL BE RUNNING OUT OF THEM SOON, RIGHT?

STIR-FRIED LIVER AND LEEKS, MY STYLE.
A MELT-IN-YOUR-MOUTH STEW OF BOK CHOY AND FILET, MY STYLE.
BONITO, LIGHTLY GRILLED, WITH CHOPPED CELERY AND PERILLA SAUCE, MY STYLE.
AND MUCH MORE.
HOW IS IT? GOOD?
...
SI LENCE
IT'S BEEN A WHILE SINCE THE FAMILY HAS HAD DINNER TOGETHER.
WAAAH!
I TRIED SO HARD TO COOK GOOD FOOD!
GLOOM
MOMMY IS SAD!!
I KEEP TELLING YOU THAT YOUR "MY STYLE" COOKING IS A BIT OFF.
I KEEP TELLING YOU NOT TO CONSIDER ME AS PART OF YOUR FAMILY.
MNCH
MNCH
...
WELL, IT'S ALL RIGHT... YOU'RE EATING IT...

...
SHK
SIF
TMP
GRIP
...
HUH?
SIF
SIF

THERE ARE THOSE WHO EXIST IN THE DARKNESS...
VAMPIRES, THOSE BEASTS IN HUMAN FORM WHO DRINK THE BLOOD FROM LIVING HUMANS...
...AND...
...VAMPIRE HUNTERS...
...THOSE WHO ARE FATED TO HUNT VAMPIRES...

VAMPIRE
KNIGHT
SEVENTH NIGHT: NIGHT PARTY

WHY ARE YOU OUTSIDE...
...DOING THIS?
NOT NOW, YUKI.
GO BACK QUICKLY AND GET YOUR WOUND TREATED.
YOUR BLOOD IS TOO PROVOCATIVE FOR US.
GRIP
B-BMP
I REALIZE...
...THERE'S STILL SO MUCH I DON'T KNOW.
SIXTH NIGHT/END

SHAA
THERE...
...WE GO.
CHAK
YOU DIDN'T NEED ME AT ALL.
YOU'RE FROM THE NIGHT CLASS ...
...TAKUMA ICHIJO AND SENRI SHIKI.
WHY ARE YOU HERE?

WHAT ?!
YOU'RE...
KREEN
KREEN

HEH HEH
?!
SHING
!

WHAT WAS THAT SOUND?
LET'S CHECK IT OUT.
THIS IS BAD.
WE CAN'T ...
BLOOD ...
HEH HEH HEH HEH HEH
...LET OTHER PEOPLE SEE THIS.
SHUM
YOU USED TO BE HUMAN.
OH?
I WON-DER.

SHUMP
ZERO!
KRAK
THE ARTEMIS ROD...
...IS UNHAPPY I'M WIELDING IT...
TUMP
SOMETHING IS HAPPENING IN THE BACK.
YEAH, IT STARTED A LITTLE WHILE AGO.
WHY IS THERE A VAMPIRE HERE?
GRIP

HUFF
LET ME...
...EAT YOU UP...
DON'T JUST STAND THERE...
...YUKI!
!!

GRIP
HEH HEH ...
GRIN
HOLD
A VAMPIRE ?!
VUP
YOUR BLOOD ...
... SMELLS GOOD ...
NO...
TRMBL

VOOSH
TUNK

ZERO?
TMP
KRK
OUCH...
OH NO ...
RIIV
ZERO!
TMP
WHERE ARE YOU ?!
ZUU ZUU

I...
...SMELL LIKE THEY DO...
OH!
KA-CHAK
ZERO....
ARE YOU ALL RIGHT?
ZERO?
WHERE DID HE GO?

ZERO.
EXCUSE ME.
ARE YOU FROM THE CROSS ACADEMY NIGHT CLASS?
?!
OH, YOU ARE!
YOU LOOK A LITTLE DIFFERENT FROM ORDINARY PEOPLE.
UM... WAIT...
STUDENTS FROM THE ELITE CLASS AREN'T LIKE EVERYONE ELSE.
SHUP
THERE'S SOMEONE NAMED AIDO IN THE NIGHT CLASS, RIGHT?
HE LIKES SWEETS, AND HE COMES HERE SOME-TIMES...
OH.
SHUP
PLEASE TELL HIM TO COME AGAIN...
I'M LEAVING.
UH...
WAIT FOR ME OUTSIDE.

HOFF
NO FAIR!
POM
SOMEHOW YOU KNOW LOTS OF THINGS ABOUT ME, ZERO...
...BUT THERE ARE LOTS OF THINGS ABOUT YOUR PAST THAT I DON'T KNOW...
...LIKE WHETHER YOU HAVE ANY BROTHERS OR SISTERS...
...OR WHICH SCHOOL YOU ATTENDED...
I HAD A YOUNGER BROTHER...
HE DIED...
...THAT DAY.

YOU STILL...
...CAN'T GO OUTSIDE SCHOOL GROUNDS ALONE...
HOFF
...
I CAN!
I KNOW YOU'RE AFRAID TO.
IF YOU GO OUTSIDE THE SCHOOL ...
...YOU REMEMBER, DON'T YOU...
...THAT NOT ALL VAMPIRES ARE "WELL-BEHAVED" LIKE KANAME KURAN...
SHUT UP!
KLANK
I'M NOT AFRAID OF WHAT HAPPENED TEN YEARS AGO.
YOU EAT A LOT.
SHMP SHMP
SLUP
SHUT UP!

EVEN IF YOU ARE...
...A VAMPIRE NOW...
...
ZERO, YOU EAT SOME-THING TOO.
I'LL TREAT YOU FOR CARRYING ALL THAT STUFF.
I WANTED TO EAT SHIO RAMEN.
WELL, I LOVE THE PARFAIT HERE, SO...
I CAN'T LOOK HIM IN THE EYE NOW...
YORI AND I CAME HERE LAST TIME...
OH!
SHE TOOK HIM TO A CAFÉ WITHOUT ASKING.

YOU LOOK LIKE A GRADE-SCHOOLER...
...AND YOU'RE ACTING LIKE A "BIG SIS"?
HA!
THAT'S HILARIOUS.
GRRRR
YOU'RE A YEAR OLDER THAN I AM, BUT YOU CUT SCHOOL-- THAT'S WHY WE'RE IN THE SAME CLASS!
WHEN WE FIRST MET, YOU WERE ABOUT THE SAME HEIGHT AS I WAS!
PLEASE GIVE ME THE CHANGE QUICKLY!
AH!
HURRY UP OR I'LL LEAVE YOU BEHIND...
I'LL TAKE THIS ONE.
YOU DON'T HAVE TO WRAP IT.
..."BIG SIS."
IT'S ONLY FOR ZERO ANY-WAY.
BEING LIKE THIS...
...MAKES ME FEEL LIKE WE'VE RETURNED TO THE OLD DAYS SOME-WHAT.
YEAH.
ZERO IS ZERO.

HEY...
GIMME YOUR ARM.
HM. GOOD.
IF I LEAVE YOU ALONE, ZERO, YOU DON'T TAKE CARE OF YOURSELF AT ALL...
YOU NEED SOMEONE TO CHOOSE FOR YOU.
YOU'RE LIKE...
HEE HEE
...A YOUNGER BROTHER WHO NEEDS LOOKING AFTER.
SWIP
OH? YOU'RE MAD.
YOU GET ANGRY SO EASILY!
I'M SO APPALLED THAT I FIND IT FUNNY.
YOU'RE A YEAR YOUNGER THAN I AM.

LU
NK..
...
OH.
HE'S COOKING FOR US.
HM. THE HEADMASTER ASKED US TO GET... LET'S SEE...
BEEF LIVER, BOK CHOY...
THERE'S MORE?
UHHH...
HEY, LOOK!
ZERO!
TUG
WE SHOULD GET BACK TO THE SCHOOL BEFORE SUNSET.
YOU DON'T HAVE TO WORRY. THE NIGHT CLASS HAS TODAY OFF SO THEY WON'T BE COMING OUT OF THEIR DORM.

MMM! ♡
IT'S BEEN A WHILE SINCE WE LAST CAME TO TOWN. ♡
IT'S A PRIVILEGE FOR THE HEADMASTER TO ASK US TO DO AN ERRAND...
...SINCE LEAVING SCHOOL GROUNDS IS RESTRICTED.
HEY!
ZERO, YOU LOOK BORED!
RIGHT NOW...
...WE SHOULD BE ENJOYING OURSELVES A LITTLE!
THERE'S NOTHING TO ENJOY.
TUG
WHAT ?!
STOP BEING SUCH A KILLJOY AND COME ON!
IT'S ALL RIGHT! YOU'LL HAVE FUN!

YOU MUST'VE BEEN REALLY WORRIED ABOUT HER.
NO WAY!
THAT WAS COLD!
...
WELL, I'M OFF TO READ MORE MANGA...
ICHIJO.
TMP
TMP
SUFF
SIGH
WHAT WOULD YOU LIKE ME TO DO...
...KANAME?

WELL... THAT SURPRISED ME.
THAT HORSE IS TOO SENSITIVE.
AS SOON AS I OPENED THE WINDOW, IT KICKED YUKI AND FREAKED OUT...
DO HERBIVORES HATE OUR SMELL THAT MUCH?
SNIFF
WHAT DO YOU THINK, KANAME?
EVEN THOUGH WE HAVE TODAY OFF...
KLAK
...YOU'RE STILL WORKING. YOU NEVER REST.
THE SENATE IS PERSISTENT IN WANTING REPORTS...
SKRITCH SKRITCH
VUNK
...
...WRITING REPORTS FOR THOSE OLD MEN EVEN THOUGH YOU DON'T WANT TO...
YOU'RE DIFFERENT FROM ME. I READ TOO MUCH MANGA, AND I'M SLEEPY DURING THE DAY.
OF COURSE.
ANYWAY, YUKI IS ALL RIGHT...
...THE HORSE ONLY KICKED HER IN THE BUTT.
PEEK
OH.
HUH?

KIRYU IS AMAZING.
HE CALMED DOWN WHITE LILY, AKA "THE WILD HORSE FROM HELL."
NO WONDER ZERO IS THE ONLY ONE IN THE DAY CLASS WHO CAN GLARE FEARLESSLY AT KANAME KURAN.
KIRYU IS THE RISING STAR OF OUR CLASS.
DAMN THOSE NIGHT CLASS GUYS!
THEY TREAT US DAY CLASS GUYS LIKE FOOLS!
ZERO!
SORRY, ZERO.
WHITE LILY IS QUICK-TEMPERED, BUT SHE'S NEVER RUN AWAY BEFORE.
I WONDER WHY SHE SUDDENLY ...
SHE PROBABLY SENSED SOMETHING SHE DIDN'T LIKE...

LILY...
SHNRR
...IT'S ALL RIGHT.
TUMP
KIRYU!
KMP

WATCH OUT, KIRYU!
KIRYU!

JUMP
KLLOMP
KLUP KLUP KLUP
SHNRRT
SHNRRT
SIGH
YOU'RE RUINING MY NAP...
KLUP
STOMP
STOMP

I

Hello to all my readers!
I was able to have vol. 2 published, despite my nervousness about drawing a serious manga... I started out in the love-comedy field, so this manga is possible because there are people who read it. I really thank you. ✿ I'm keeping my editor uneasy... (I'm sorry, Ide-sama... 👌)

I tried hard on drawing new stuff. In Volume 1, I complained that I couldn't make fun of the serious *Vampire Knight*! But I did a lot of it at the end of this volume, yes. Moreover, the side stories are not serious at all, so if you're really into serious stuff, it may be a little hard to read it? ↑(Fainthearted...) But there is a wonderful word called "diversion" too, so I hope you can enjoy things together with me. Defiant attitude!

◆

By the way, the blood-covered arm of the Sixth Night... I wonder whose it is? ←(Don't ask.) I drew it thinking... "Who is this...?"

I JUST ...
I HAD SOME-THING ON MY MIND...
...
I HAVE... BAD NEWS FOR YOU, YUKI.
SHNRRT
YOU WERE ASLEEP ...
...SO NOW THE ONLY HORSE LEFT FOR YOUR LESSON...
...IS WHITE LILY, THE WILD HORSE.
VAM
I'M DONE WITH MY LESSON...
PAT
...SO USE YOUR GUTS AND RIDE, YUKI.
IF YOU LOOK AWAY, SHE WILL KICK YOU.
O... OKAY ...
TMP
TMP
EASY, THERE ...
SHP
VAM

...A MAD VAMPIRE ...
...LUSTING FOR BLOOD.
YUKI, WAKE UP!
GRIP
... YORI!
IT'S UNUSUAL FOR YOU TO FALL ASLEEP DURING PHYS ED.

IT'S ZERO'S DECISION...
NOD
HA HA HA HA!
YOU LOOK LIKE A DORK!
YOU, OVER THERE! BE SERIOUS!
TEN YEARS AGO...
...THAT MAN WAS THERE...

NOT YET...
...BUT THAT DAY WILL EVENTUALLY COME.
KILL ME BY YOUR OWN HAND THEN.
ZERO...
...IS AFRAID OF GOING BERSERK AND BECOMING A VAMPIRE WHO ONLY LUSTS AFTER BLOOD...

SIXTH NIGHT: OUTSIDE CROSS ACADEMY
VAMPIRE
KNIGHT

VAMPIRE KNIGHT™

Contents

Sixth Night: Outside Cross Academy.................5
Seventh Night: Night Party.............................38
Eighth Night: The Forbidden Act....................90
Ninth Night: Choices Made...........................122
Sometimes There Are Lazy Days Too............159
I Must've Been Born Under the "Victim of Circumstances" Star...175
Vampires Covered in Blood Are Prohibited from Entering This Page!!.............................180
Editor's Notes..188

3 Zero had actually been bitten by a pureblood vampire!

For four years, Zero had been resisting his vampire instincts, suffering greatly. But he eventually sinks his fangs into Yuki! Zero blames himself and tries to leave the school, but Yuki stops him, deciding to be his ally...

※ Pureblood vampires are vampires who do not have a single drop of human blood in their lineage. They are very powerful, and they can turn humans into vampires by drinking their blood.

KANAME KURAN
Night Class President and pureblood vampire. Yuki adores him.

YUKI CROSS
The heroine.
The adopted daughter of the Headmaster, and a Guardian who protects Cross Academy.

ZERO KIRYU
Yuki's childhood friend and a Guardian.
His family was killed by a vampire a very long time ago.

YORI
Yuki's best friend.

HEADMASTER CROSS
He raised Yuki.
He is trying to educate the students to become a bridge between humans and vampires.

HANABUSA AIDO
Nickname: Idol

AKATSUKI KAIN
Nickname: Wild

What is to be their fate?!

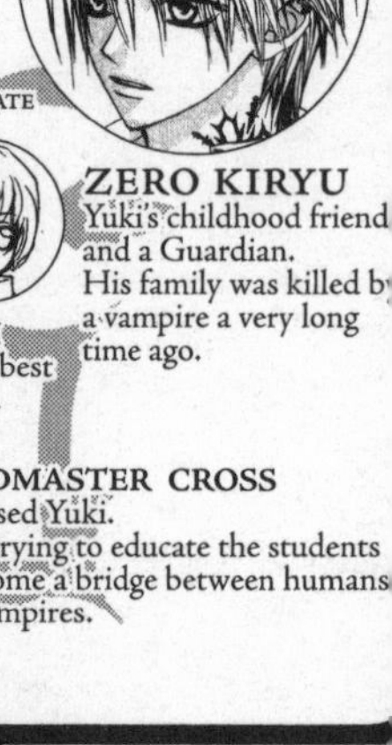

The Story of VAMPIRE KNIGHT

1 Cross Academy, the distinguished private boarding school, has a Day Class for ordinary students and a Night Class for vampires.

The elite Night Class students are all vampires!

The existence of vampires and the truth behind the Night Class is kept secret from Day Class students, who unknowingly coexist with them.

2 Yuki is the adopted daughter of the Headmaster of Cross Academy. She has no memories of herself prior to age 5. Zero loathes vampires after his family was killed by one. The two childhood friends are School Guardians who protect the secret of the Night Class!

VAMPIRE KNIGHT™

Story & Art by
Matsuri Hino

Vol. 2